Happy Holidays

from your

Colleagues on Call

John Antonetti & Jim Garver

Teachers Have Class...

JUST ASK THE KIDS!

Suzanne Zenkel

 Peter Pauper Press, Inc.
White Plains, New York

Dedication

Dedicated to all the extraordinary teachers at Central School,
who really are in a class by themselves.

Acknowledgments

Special thanks go to Lydia Kelley and Januari Pakrul and to all the
great kids whose creative, thoughtful, and clever
contributions fill the pages of this book.
—SSZ

Peter Pauper Press also gratefully acknowledges the help of
Connie Burchett and Rasheen Hewlett, and the kids at
Lakeview Elementary School and Lincoln School.

Designed by Rebecca Lown
Illustrations by Elaine Lopez
Endpaper artwork by Jeremy Levine

Copyright © 2009
Peter Pauper Press, Inc.
202 Mamaroneck Avenue
White Plains, NY 10601
All rights reserved
ISBN 978-1-59359-833-4
Printed in China
7   6   5   4   3   2   1

Visit us at www.peterpauper.com

Teachers
Have Class...

JUST ASK THE KIDS!

Contents

Introduction

Got Class? Sure you do, you're a teacher! And your class is filled with kids who love and admire you, sometimes for the most unimaginable reasons!

We surveyed a diverse group of more than 150 kids, ages five to eleven, asking them 11 basic questions about their teachers. Their responses were sometimes surprising, often hilarious, and uniformly endearing. Like the students themselves, their comments were warm and disarmingly witty, sometimes remarkably candid—but always illuminating and instructive.

Sometimes the lessons we learn from children are the most valuable because their insights are fresh, free from the weight of a lifetime of baggage. Their thoughts come straight from the heart. And they make an awful lot of good sense.

The responses in this book are just highlights from the many answers we received. But one point comes across loud and clear: Teachers should never underestimate the incredible power of their compassion and good humor. Children decidedly do remember the times when you were there for them, and the impact of your actions is lasting and inestimable.

So here it is, in their own words. The scoop from your kids, up front and personal. A report card that comes straight from the heart.

What do you like best about your teacher?

"I like that my teacher helps you when you're sad or have a problem."

—Jenn, age 10

"Sometimes she gives us extra recess."

—Gabriel, age 9

"My teacher is bubbly and thinks like a kid."

—Tia, age 10

(7)

"She can rock."
—Sabrina, age 10

What do you like best about your teacher?

"She makes us smart."
—Brianna, age 7

"She's spiffy."
—Isabella, age 9

"She loves us."
—Samiah, age 6

Is there anything you don't like about your teacher? If so, what?

Mrs. Carter's
Third Grade
Class

"Um, no not really because even when she's serious she's gentle and doesn't make it seem too harsh."

—*Grace, age 8*

"No, if she was fired, I would tell the Principal not to fire her."

—*Emily, age 5*

"I like everything about her."

—Georgette, age 9

"I don't like it when my teacher doesn't call on me when I raise my hand."

—Savanna, age 8

"Her phone rings too much. P.S. She has a great ring tone."

—Steven, age 10

If your teacher were an animal, what animal would he or she be, and why?

Mrs. Robin's Fourth Grade Class

(15)

If your teacher were an animal, what animal would he or she be, and why?

"A monkey because she is fun and so are monkeys."

—Molly, age 8

"She would be an elephant. She protects her students like they're her children."

—Josy, age 9

"My teacher would be a rabbit because she hears EVERYTHING!"

—Patrick, age 11

A+

"A koo koo bird because sometimes she does koo koo things."

—Emily, age 5

"A swan because she is graceful."

—Stephen, age 9

"A penguin because she wears black and white."

—Victor, age 10

"A cow because she is a Dallas Cowboys fan."

—Anthony, age 7

"She'd be a cat because she's always nice and never jumps up on people."

—Lucy, age 7

(19)

"A gorilla because they are smart and my teacher is smart."

—Gianfranco, age 7

If you could be teacher for a day, what would you do?

Miss Adams
2nd Grade

If you could be teacher for a day, what would you do?

"Let pets come to school."

—Molly, age 10

"Let them do their homework in class so they could play after school."

—Alec, age 7

"I would teach kids what I learned from my teacher."

—Jazlyn, age 7

If you could be teacher for a day, what would you do?

"Give myself a day off!"

—Gideon, age 7

"I would put music on, do a dance party, but still do math."

—Grace, age 8

"Give free nachos and make it recess ALL day. No homework!"

—Harrison, age 9

If you could be teacher for a day, what would you do?

"Art."

— Al, age 10

"Make all the kids make me the biggest ice cream sundae ever."

— Alex, age 10

"We would read, have art, have snack and then do a lot of crazy science experiments."

— Grace, age 10

"Go home."

— Emma, age 6

What's the difference between teachers and parents?

Mrs. Wheeler
Grade 3

"The teacher teaches. The parent makes the food."

—Nick, age 7

"My mom tells me to take out the garbage and my teacher doesn't."

—Gabriella, age 6

"My mom and dad don't teach me anything."

—Caroline, age 10

STONE ELEM SCHOOL
GRADE 1P   APR 65

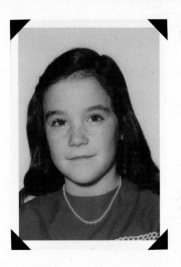

"Your teacher doesn't own you."

—Isabel, age 7

(29)

What's the difference between teachers and parents?

"Teachers don't yell at you to clean your room."

—Josy, age 9

"I'd say parents don't teach much and teachers teach you more."

—Vanessa, age 9

"Parents really take care of you and teachers give your brain more knowledge."

—Grace, age 8

"My dad is brown and my teacher is white."

—Grant, age 6

What's the difference between teachers and parents?

"Teachers have a teachers' lounge and parents have a living room."

—Steven, age 9

"A teacher is really important."

—Clare, age 8

"Teachers are smarter than parents."

—Gregory, age 10

What's the difference between teachers and parents?

"Teachers give you homework. Parents give you presents."

—Katelyn, age 10

"You were born with your mom. Your teacher wasn't there that day."

—Samantha, age 9

"Parents live with you and teachers teach with you."

—Kaitlin, age 6

"Teachers can't ground you!"

—Courtney, age 11

What do you think your teacher does after school?

(33)

"E-mail, work,
schedules tomorrow and
tomorrow's homework."

—Caroline, age 10

"Eats a snack."

—Daniel, age 6

"My teacher offers to help kids after school so it does not take away from the regular class time."

—Jacqueline, age 11

What do you think your teacher does after school?

"Watches *Lost* and types."

—Drew, age 7

"She goes home and naps."

—Tyler, age 8

"She goes home and teaches her kids."

—Mia, age 7

"She cleans the class."

—Ava, age 7

A+

What do you think your teacher does after school?

"Corrects homework, goes to Dunkin' Donuts, and hangs out with friends and family."

—Al, age 10

"Parties all night long."

—Vitoria, age 9

"Does acupuncture on Thursdays."

—Alex, age 10

"Thanks God the kids are gone."

—Matthew, age 9

What's the funniest thing about your teacher?

What's the funniest thing about your teacher?

"My teacher is not funniest."

—Michael, age 5

"She has a funny laugh."

—Jogis, age 10

"She cracks jokes."

—John, age 8

"She plays tag with us on the roof even though she's old and not supposed to."

—Jack, age 8

What's the funniest thing about your teacher?

"My teacher calls me wonder nugget."

—Dylan, age 7

"She dances with us at the end of almost every day."

—Katie, age 10

What's the funniest thing about your teacher?

"She scrunches up her nose when she laughs."

—Olivia, age 10

"When my teacher acts out people in a book we're reading."

—Jacqueline, age 11

"That her nickname is Pickle."

—Tommy, age 10

"She wore a funny cook outfit and gross teeth for her Halloween costume."

—Kaitlin, age 6

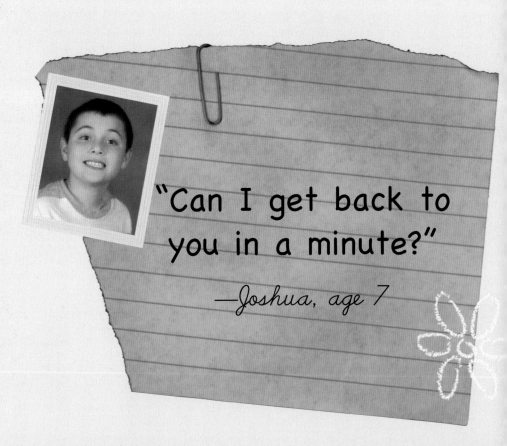

"Can I get back to you in a minute?"

—Joshua, age 7

What's the best gift you could give your teacher?

"New boots and a Mustang."

—*Tommy, age 10*

"I'd say an apple. I gave her an apple once and she said it's the best gift she ever had."

—*Vanessa, age 9*

"The best gift you could give your teacher is something you made yourself."

—*Grace, age 10*

(47)

"Mick Jagger from the Rolling Stones."

—*Victoria, age 10*

"Books."

—*John, age 8*

"A gift card to a shoe store."

—*Kaitlin, age 6*

"A surprise party in class when it's her birthday."

—Charlie, age 7

(49)

What's the best gift you could give your teacher?

"A toy."

—Sassy, age 5

"Having me in 4th grade in her class forever."

—Grace, age 10

"Homemade cookies."

—Jumee, age 7

"A big hug."

—Annie, age 6

"I would give her a flower."

—Nina, age 8

"Everything, she's the best."

—Amanda, age 10

"A day off."

—David, age 10

What's the most important thing you've learned from your teacher?

What's the most important thing you've learned from your teacher?

"You learn more when you listen."

— Isabella, age 9

"Manners."

— Josy, age 9

"How to hold my pencil properly."

— Lucy, age 7

"Never be mean."

— Gideon, age 7

"Not to talk to strangers."

—Valentina, age 7

"There's something called TRUCK. It's Trust, Respect, Understanding, Courtesy, and Kindness."

—Olivia, age 10

What's the most important thing you've learned from your teacher?

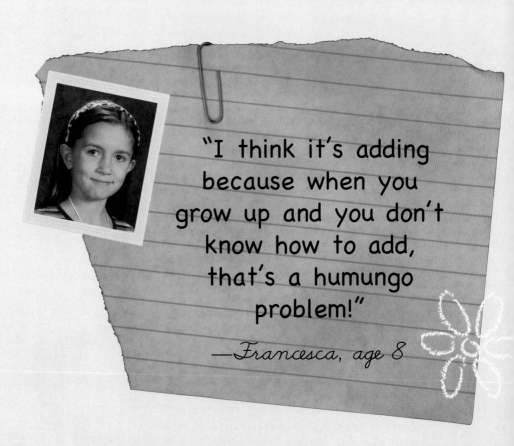

"I think it's adding because when you grow up and you don't know how to add, that's a humungo problem!"

—Francesca, age 8

What's the most important thing you've learned from your teacher?

"Don't run in the hall."

—Rebecca, age 7

"A LOT! That's why she's soooooooooo cool."

—Alana, age 10

"Never make fun of what people eat."

—Steven, age 9

"The most important thing that I learned from my teacher is to be your own best friend."

—Mohit, age 10

"Mind your biznes."

—Kevin, age 7

What's the nicest thing your teacher has done for you?

(59)

What's the nicest thing your teacher has done for you?

"She gave me another chance."

—*Lily, age 7*

"Listens to me when I talk."

—*Katelyn, age 10*

"She lets me draw when I want."

—*Benny, age 10*

"Stayed up with me at lunch so I could catch up."

—*Caroline, age 10*

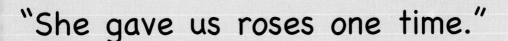

"She gave us roses one time."

—Violet, age 8

What's the nicest thing your teacher has done for you?

"She makes us happy when we feel sad."

—Will, age 7

"When I struggle she helps me."

—Jacqueline, age 11

"She is letting me write sloppy because I broke my wrist."

—Alec, age 7

What's the nicest thing your teacher has done for you?

"When she compliments my work, it makes me feel special."

—Tia, age 10

"Whenever I go home sick, she always says, 'Feel better,' and when I come back she asks if I'm OK."

—Olivia, age 10

"When we're hot and we just came inside from recess or gym she sometimes goes and gets us a drink at the water thingy."

—Mason, age 6

MAYFIELD SCHOOL

ROCKVILLE, FLORIDA

GRADE 2 1965-66

(64)

What's the nicest thing
your teacher
has done for you?

"Hugs."

—Charlotte, age 6

Do you want to be a teacher when you grow up? (Why or why not?)

"I do want to be a teacher because you get to go to the teachers' lounge and you get to have laughs with the kids."

—Jogis, age 10

"I do not because I am looking into another job."

—Tom, age 10

(67)

Do you want to be a teacher when you grow up? (Why or why not?)

"Yes! Because I love being a kid and I don't want to grow up and if you are a teacher, you get to be with kids' stuff and talk to kids all day!"

—Sarah, age 11

"No I want to get out of school as fast as possible."

—Matthew, age 9

"No because I want to do microbiology and zoology and I don't like teaching. I've tried it."

—*Alex, age 10*

"No, because I want to be a soccer player. Actually, I want to be a teacher that plays soccer. A teacher that teaches their kids how to play soccer, actually. And I'm going to be a soccer player."

—*Mason, age 6*

Do you want to be a teacher when you grow up? (Why or why not?)

"No. I want to be a rock star."

—Sabrina, age 10

"Yes, because I think it's cool."

—Ali, age 9

"Yes! Because you get to be the boss!"

—Clare, age 8

"Yes because it is fun."

—Kayla, age 6

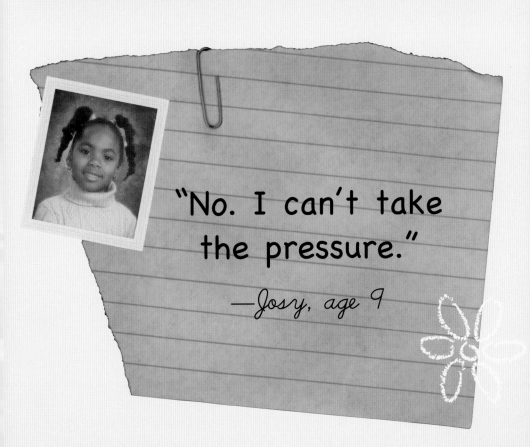

"No. I can't take the pressure."

—Josy, age 9

"Yes because I want to be just like my teacher."

—Jumee, age 7